# POSSESS YOUR PROMISED LAND

LEARN TO DEFEAT YOUR HIDDEN ENEMIES

# FUCHSIA PICKETT

Charisma
HOUSE
A STRANG COMPANY

POSSESS YOUR PROMISED LAND by Fuchsia Pickett
Published by Charisma House
A part of Strang Communications Company
600 Rinehart Road
Lake Mary, Florida 32746
www.charismahouse.com

Cover design by Rachel Campbell
Interior typography by Sallie Traynor

Library of Congress Cataloging-in-Publication Data

Pickett, Fuchsia T.
  Possess your promised land / Fuchsia Pickett.
      p. cm.
Includes bibliographical references and index.
  ISBN 0-88419-966-5
  1. Spiritual warfare. I. Title.
BV4509.5 .P54 2003
248.4--dc21

2003010796

03 04 05 06 07 — 87654321
Printed in the United States of America

Faithful friends are truly a gift from God.
Tommy and Judy Weatherford have
proven to be that to Leroy and me.
To this special couple I dedicate this book.

# Contents

Chapter 1

# God's Promise

*Let us hold fast the profession of our*
*faith without wavering; (for he is*
*faithful that promised;).*
—Hebrews 10:23, kjv

1

U nless you have a clear understanding of what your promised land is, you will not be motivated to do what is necessary to pursue it and possess it. To have the passion needed to secure your promised land successfully, you will need a clear understanding of its relevance to your life today as well as its eternal benefits.

What do you think of when you hear the term *promised land*? An Old Testament place somewhere in the Middle East? A homeland for Israel? Heaven? Your personal destiny?

Although those may be correct answers in certain contexts, it can be difficult, as a twenty-first century Christian, to apply the term *promised land* to your personal life. As you begin to explore the plan God has for you to inherit your personal promised land, you first need to understand the significance of the term so that you can be filled with the passion and desire to receive your divine inheritance.

> *The fact that almost all the promises in the Bible were made by God to man indicates that God's nature is characterized chiefly by grace and faithfulness.*

Let's begin with the word *promise*. According to *Nelson's Illustrated Bible Dictionary,* the biblical use of *promise* reveals the grace of God to man. It means, "a solemn pledge to perform or grant a specified thing."[1] God did not have to promise anything to sinful man. But the fact that almost all the promises in the Bible were made by God to man indicates that God's nature is characterized chiefly by grace and faithfulness. Grace prompted God to promise a new land to the Israelites (Exod. 12:25). His faithfulness urged Him to fulfill that promise in spite of the nation's disobedience. And as Paul pointed out in Galatians 3:15–29, God's faithfulness and grace are particularly evident in His promise to Abraham.

## God's Promise to Abraham

Abraham was a man chosen by God to be the father of a holy nation. As Abraham obeyed the word of the Lord, God continued to unfold His plan for the nation of Israel. Somehow, God's divine plan for Abraham became the passion of Abraham's heart as well, as seen in his radical obedience to the commands of God. God promised that Abraham's seed would be more than the sand of the sea and the stars of the sky. He promised Abraham a land that would be set apart for the nation he was to become.

When Abraham became an old man and still did not have an heir, he agonized with God regarding the fulfillment of His promise to give him a son. And the Scriptures declare that when God did give him the son of promise, Isaac, and then required Abraham to offer him as a sacrifice, Abraham believed that he would receive him back from the dead if necessary so that the promise of God could be fulfilled (Heb. 11:17–19).

It is difficult to imagine the relationship God enjoyed with Abraham, a man whom He called His friend, declaring that He would do nothing that He did not first discuss with this faithful man (James 2:23; Gen. 18:17). The keys to Abraham's receiving the Promised Land of God by faith, though he died without possessing it, lie deep in the heart reality of this divine relationship. Personal ambition, desire for ministry, or other lesser motivating forces commonly attributed to our twenty-first century lives did not motivate Abraham to live the life of sacrificial obedience that the Scriptures reveal. Though his life was far from perfect, his passion for life was his personal relationship with God, who reckoned it as righteousness (James 2:23).

Understanding God's promises for your life and discovering divine purpose and personal destiny will also be a result of personal relationship with God. An intellectual acceptance or superficial obedience to religious duty will not motivate you to possess your promised land. You will not progress past the wilderness of wandering that cost an entire generation of Israelites their lives unless you discover the keys of relationship with God that Abraham, Moses, Joshua, Caleb and other Bible heroes experienced.

Even after we leave "Egypt," the land that typifies

our bondage to sin, there is no guarantee that we will possess the land of freedom and abundance God promised His people. But God is faithful, and He will reveal to us the way we should walk to discover His purpose for our lives and enter our promised land as we decide to follow Him wholeheartedly. Scripture testifies of Caleb:

> But My servant Caleb, because he has had a different spirit and has followed Me fully, I will bring into the land which he entered, and his descendants shall take possession of it.
>
> —NUMBERS 14:24

As we explore the requirements for possessing your promised land, you will continually see that submitting to the lordship of Christ in your life—following Him fully—represents the first prerequisite. Cultivating relationship, developing desire and becoming equipped to inherit the promise of God for your life all hinge upon your primary decision to abandon yourself to the lordship of Christ. Men like Caleb and Joshua, the commander of Israel who led them into the Promised Land, must become role models in this regard. You will need to exhibit the spirit of

*Understanding God's promises for your life and discovering divine purpose and personal destiny will be a result of personal relationship with God.*

Abraham, whom the New Testament calls our father in the faith, if you are to receive the promises that he did. When God called Abraham, He made clear the requirements for his obedience:

> Now the LORD said to Abram [Abraham], "Go forth from your country, and from your relatives and from your father's house, to the land which I will show you; and I will make you a great nation, and I will bless you, and make your name great; and so you shall be a blessing; and I will bless those who bless you, and the one who curses you I will curse. And in you all the families of the earth shall be blessed."
>
> —GENESIS 12:1–3

A careful reading of Abraham's requirements for following God makes us aware of their stark resemblance to the requirements Jesus gave His disciples for following Him:

> If anyone comes to Me, and does not hate his own father and mother and wife and children and brothers and sisters, yes, and even his own life, he cannot be My disciple. Whoever does not carry his own cross and come after Me cannot be My disciple.
>
> —LUKE 14:26–27

Loving God above all earthly attachments and becoming willing to forsake all else in utter abandonment to the will of God is clearly required of all who desire to inherit their promised land.

## God's Promise to Moses

Hundreds of years after Abraham, God's chosen people had multiplied greatly during a period of more than four hundred years of bondage and slavery in the land of Egypt. Again, God chose a man and spoke to him regarding the land He had promised Abraham to give to his descendants. As we read of the Exodus of these slaves from the only life they had known under Pharaoh, it is difficult to grasp the awe of the mighty deliverance they experienced at the hand of Almighty God.

They were a multitude, but not yet a nation; they were free from the oppression of slavery, but not yet equipped to enjoy their freedom. Their murmuring and complaining against their leaders, their supernatural provisions of food and the rigors of wilderness wandering finally cost them their lives. That generation died without entering the Promised Land that God had promised to give to them.

*God's desire was not only to deliver His people from the bondage that physically enslaved them, but also to bring them into the blessing He had promised hundreds of years earlier to their father Abraham.*

God's promise did not change; His plan was not only to take them out of their life of slavery, but also to take them into the Promised Land. But they failed as a people to submit to the government of God for them, angering God in their rebellion to the point of making Him want to destroy them. Moses had to intercede on their behalf before God to spare their lives. Have you ever wondered why they did not experience a turning of their hearts to faith in their Deliverer, God Himself, and in His servant Moses? And why were Joshua and Caleb filled with faith to receive the promise of God, even though they saw firsthand the enemies in the land of Canaan whom they would have to defeat?

Answers to these questions will serve you well in your pursuit of the purposes of God—your promised land. They will give you the keys that will unlock the promises of God for your life as they did for God's faithful servants.

## GOD'S PROMISE TO JOSHUA

The Book of Joshua describes the conquest of the land of Canaan—the Promised Land—under the leadership of Joshua, Moses' successor. Joshua had been an excellent understudy of Moses throughout the forty years of wandering in the wilderness. He was with Moses at Mount Sinai when Moses received the Ten Commandments (Exod. 24:13). He was one of the twelve spies (Num. 13:8, 16). Joshua was indeed a great man of tremendous faith, courage and leadership ability who believed that God would do what He promised.

The deliverance that was begun in the Book of Exodus was completed in the Book of Joshua. Joshua was victorious in destroying the Canaanites because of a new breed of Israelite, those who took God at His word. The main purpose of the Book of Joshua was to show how God kept His original promise to Abraham and how the wicked were expelled.[2]

The deliverance from their *external* bondage of slavery in Egypt was only the beginning of the deliverance for the children of Israel. Changing their leadership and their lifestyle was preparation for receiving the promises of God both individually and as a nation. Yet their wilderness journey revealed all manner of inner bondage to attitudes of rebellion, unbelief, fear and anger. God, who graciously accompanied them with His presence in the cloud by day and the pillar of fire by night, would have delivered them of these bondages as well if they had chosen to submit to His ways.

*There is always a time element involved in the promises of God for our lives.*

We have to believe this is true because of the testimony of those who chose to obey God wholly—such as Caleb and Joshua. We know also that it was God's plan to take the Israelites into the Promised Land; this required that they give up their unbelief and trust His delivering power, which they had witnessed so forcefully in Egypt. God's desire was not only to deliver His people from the bondage that physically enslaved them, but also to bring them into the blessing He had promised hundreds of years earlier to their father Abraham.

Through Abraham's obedience, he received the promise and beheld the Promised Land; yet it was for an appointed time in the future that his descendants would possess it. And it would be through obedience again that Israel would possess the land. When Stephen recounted the story of his people, just before he was martyred for his faith, he rehearsed this time element involved in God's promise to Abraham:

> But as the time of the promise was approaching which God had assured to Abraham, the people increased and multiplied in Egypt.
> —ACTS 7:17

There is always a time element involved in the promises of God for our lives. We must be careful not to allow unbelief to grow during a time period that seems to delay the promise of God. God uses time as a tool for the testing of our hearts to bring us into dependence on His supernatural power and childlike trust in His ways.

How the hearts of Caleb and Joshua must have been tested during their wanderings in the desert those forty years. They believed that God would help them defeat the enemies in the Promised Land so that they could possess it. Yet they were forced to wander with the multitude of Israelites who did not believe God's promise. Only after all the unbelieving souls died in that wilderness and God took the life of Moses, their leader, did God tell Joshua that it was time to enter the Promised Land. It was now up to Joshua to obey His commands in order to receive the promise of God for His people:

*Everything that happened to Israel was for our example.*

> Moses My servant is dead; now therefore arise, cross this Jordan, you and all this people, to the land which I am giving to them, to the sons of Israel. Every place on which the sole of your foot treads, I have given it to you, just as I spoke to Moses…No man will be able to stand before you all the days of your life. Just as I have been with Moses, I will be with you; I will not fail you or forsake you. Be strong and courageous, for you shall give this people possession of the land which I swore to their fathers to give them.
>
> —JOSHUA 1:2–3, 5–6

God reassured Joshua once again that He was giving this land to the children of Israel. Though He commanded Joshua to arise and cross the Jordan with the people, it was God Himself who would give them the land. He promised to be with Joshua as He had been with Moses. God's part was the supernatural intervention that made it possible for His people to possess the Promised Land. Joshua's part was to obey God's commands and to be courageous in the face of the battles that would ensue. God's purpose for war would eventually become apparent to these people. War was not only necessary to rid the land of their enemies, but it would also do a redemptive work in their own hearts.

## GOD'S PROMISE TO YOU

As we continue to look at these historical events regarding Israel's process of possessing the Promised Land, we need to understand how to apply the principles they learned to our own lives. It was the apostle Paul who declared that everything that happened to Israel was for our example:

> For I do not want you to be unaware, brethren, that our fathers were all under the cloud, and all passed through the sea; and all were baptized into Moses in the cloud and in the sea; and all ate the same spiritual food; and all drank the same spiritual drink, for they were drinking from a spiritual rock which followed them; and the rock was Christ. Nevertheless, with most of them God was not well-pleased; for they were laid low in the wilderness. Now these things happened as examples for us, that we should not crave evil things, as they also craved.
> —1 CORINTHIANS 10:1–6

The children of Israel all experienced baptism in type by passing under the cloud and through the sea. And the apostle Paul boldly declared that Christ was the Rock from which they drank. He understood the typology of Israel's natural historical events, which represent the spiritual work of salvation through Christ in our lives. And he warned New Testament Christians who were baptized in Christ and following Him that they could be guilty of the same wickedness that overthrew the Israelites in the wilderness:

> And do not be idolaters, as some of them were; as it is written, "The people sat down to eat and drink, and stood up to play." Nor let us act immorally, as some of them did, and twenty-three thousand fell in one day. Nor let us try the Lord, as some of them did, and were destroyed by the serpents. Nor grumble, as some of them did, and were destroyed by the destroyer. Now these things happened to them as an example, and they were written for our instruction, upon whom the ends of the ages have come.
>
> —1 Corinthians 10:7–11

After warning his fellow believers of the danger of not inheriting their promised land because of their own wickedness, Paul quickly reminded them of the faithfulness of God to His promise:

> No temptation has overtaken you but such as is common to man; and God is faithful, who

Why didn't God overwhelm the enemies of Israel before they arrived at Canaan so His people could just walk in and settle down after their years of wandering in the desert? Surely a few plagues like those He visited on the Egyptians to deliver His people from slavery would have cleared the Promised Land of their enemies. You may wonder why you have to face threatening enemies in your own life as well that can keep you from inheriting your promised land.

In His wisdom, God arranged every confrontation of Israel with the powerful enemies who occupied the land of Canaan. Israel had to dispossess them in order to inherit the Promised Land. Relationship with their God is the paramount goal of God for His people. He understood that the battles the Israelites would face to receive their inheritance would nurture that relationship.

Under the capable leadership of Joshua, their obedience to the commands of God would not only defeat their enemies, but it would also strengthen their trust and confidence in God. In gratitude for the supernatural victories they would experience and the rewards they would receive, they would worship their God and build memorials for generations

> *Relationship with their God is the paramount goal of God for His people.*

that followed to remember. Their obedience to God and their dependency on His Word, as well as His delivering power, would establish their relationship with a holy God.

Another reason God left the enemies in the land was to give the people a chance to grow so that they could inherit the promise. He declared to Moses:

> I will not drive them out from before you in one year, lest the land become desolate and the beasts of the field become too numerous for you. Little by little I will drive them out from before you, until you have increased, and you inherit the land.
>
> —Exodus 23:29–30

The enemies in the land actually served a purpose to keep the land from becoming desolate so that the beasts of the field would not overrun it until Israel could fully occupy it. One Bible commentator concludes:

> The wisdom of God is to be observed in the gradual advances of the church's interests. It is in real kindness to the church that its enemies are subdued little by little; for thus we are kept upon our guard, and in a continual dependence upon God. Corruptions are thus driven out of the hearts of God's people; not all at once, but little by little; the old man is crucified, and therefore dies slowly. God, in his providence, often delays mercies, because we are not ready for them.[1]

Your commitment to inherit your promised land cannot be accomplished in a day or even a year. Life continues to present challenges to you that are meant for your growth and maturity and to develop your dependency on God. For you, as for Israel, God's paramount goal is relationship with Him. If you could realize that and understand that relationship with God—knowing Him—is your ultimate benefit in life, you would soon be gripped with the passion necessary to abandon yourself to His will, no matter what the cost. According to Scripture, all of life's trials have the same purpose from God's perspective:

> Consider it all joy, my brethren, when you encounter various trials, knowing that the testing of your faith produces endurance. And let endurance have its perfect result, that you may be perfect and complete, lacking in nothing.
>
> —JAMES 1:2–4

> Beloved, do not be surprised at the fiery ordeal among you, which comes upon you for your testing, as though some strange thing were happening to you; but to the degree that you share the sufferings of Christ, keep on rejoicing; so that also at the revelation of His glory, you may rejoice with exultation.
>
> —1 PETER 4:12–13

It is difficult to know what is in your heart. The Bible indicates that is not even possible, declaring,

"The heart is deceitful above all things, and desperately wicked: who can know it?" (Jer. 17:9, KJV). So God in His wisdom ordains circumstances and situations that will test your heart and show you what is there that is not pleasing to Him. When you repent of those things, you become more like Christ.

*Your commitment to inherit your promised land cannot be accomplished in a day or even a year.*

God also tests your heart to see if you will obey His commands. He knows that only in obedience to Him can you inherit your promised land. He made this clear to His chosen people:

> All the commandments that I am commanding you today you shall be careful to do, that you may live and multiply, and go in and possess the land which the LORD swore to give to your forefathers. And you shall remember all the way which the LORD your God has led you in the wilderness these forty years, that He might humble you, testing you, to know what was in your heart, whether you would keep His commandments or not. And He humbled you and let you be hungry, and fed you with manna which you did not know, nor did your fathers know, that He might make you understand that man does not live by bread

alone, but man lives by everything that pro-
ceeds out of the mouth of the LORD.
—DEUTERONOMY 8:1–3

Even God's miracles, like the manna He fed His
people daily in the wilderness, have the larger purpose of humbling us to teach us the reality of our
dependency on our relationship with God. He tests
us to see if we will obey His commandments,
knowing that only if we do can we inherit our
promised land.

God even left nations in the land of Canaan for the
next generation to have to fight:

Now these are the nations which the LORD left,
to test Israel by them (that is, all who had not
experienced any of the wars of Canaan; only
in order that the generations of the sons of
Israel might be taught war, those who had not
experienced it formerly).
—JUDGES 3:1–2

Is God interested in perpetuating war? No. He
simply knows that warfare is necessary for you to
receive your inheritance because of the real enemies
that you face who are determined to keep you
from it. If you carefully obey His commands,
you will always be victorious over your enemies and
will enter into the promises of God for which you
have been willing to do battle. Jesus Himself taught
this principle to His followers:

And from the days of John the Baptist until

now the kingdom of heaven suffers violence,
and violent men take it by force.
>                                    —MATTHEW 11:12

As you accept God's purpose for war, yielding to
the redemptive work it does in your heart to allow
you to receive your
inheritance and ful-
fill your destiny, you
will soon become
aware of the prepa-
rations necessary to
engage victoriously
in those battles. God
gave Joshua certain
commands that the
people had to obey to prepare for entering
the Promised Land. Obedience to those commands
was imperative if they were to be successful in
their quest.

> *Even God's miracles have the larger purpose of humbling us to teach us the reality of our dependency on our relationship with God.*

*Chapter 3*

# Preparation for War

*Only be strong and very courageous;*
*be careful to do according to all the law . . .*
*do not turn from it to the right or to the*
*left, so that you may have success*
*wherever you go.*
—Joshua 1:7

The mood of the Israelites must have been upbeat; the people were filled with anticipation of finally entering the Promised Land that they had heard about since they were children. Moses, who had led them to this point, was dead, and Joshua was their new leader. He had heard from God. That was evident from the commands he was giving the people, telling them:

> Prepare provisions for yourselves, for within three days you are to cross this Jordan, to go in to possess the land which the LORD your God is giving you, to possess it.
> —JOSHUA 1:11

Joshua continued giving specific commands to each tribe, and the people responded favorably:

> And they answered Joshua, saying, "All that you have commanded us we will do, and wherever you send us we will go."
> —JOSHUA 1:16

There were still some significant events that had to unfold before this fledgling nation could begin to possess the Promised Land. Strategically, Joshua sent two spies into the land to view the enemy and bring back their "intelligence" briefing. Thankfully, these two men returned with a faith-filled report, saying, "Surely the LORD has given all the land into our hands, and all the inhabitants of the land, moreover, have melted away before us" (Josh. 2:24).

## SUPERNATURAL PASSAGE

Then Joshua prepared the people to cross the Jordan River. He gave them specific instructions regarding the order of the crossing. The ark of the covenant of the Lord was to go first, and everyone was to stay well behind it in order to see where it went. The warning was clear: "That you may know the way by which you shall go, for you have not passed this way before" (Josh. 3:4). Of course, the ark, carried by the priests, represented the guidance of God without which they could not proceed. It is an easy lesson to understand: Even though God is giving you your inheritance, you must take care to follow His leading in order to possess it.

There was no hope of crossing the Jordan River without supernatural intervention to open a pathway in the midst of it. Once again, faith was required in order to approach this impossibility that only God could remove. When the priests took that step into the waters with the ark of the covenant, the Bible says, "The waters which were flowing down from above stood and rose up in one heap, a great distance away...and those which were flowing

> *Even though God is giving you your inheritance, you must take care to follow His leading in order to possess it.*

down toward the sea…were completely cut off"
(Josh. 3:16).

Have you noticed another startling miracle that
took place here? The priests who carried the ark
stood firm on dry ground in the middle of the
Jordan while the nation crossed on dry ground
(v. 17). No riverbed would consist of "dry ground"
without days or weeks of being exposed to the air.
Yet, as soon as the priests entered the waters, the
river stopped flowing, and the ground provided dry
passage for the entire nation. God was giving them
their Promised Land, indeed.

### Creating a memorial

God spoke to Joshua again after the Israelites had
crossed over the Jordan River. He gave him specific
instructions for creating a memorial to His supernatural intervention. This memorial was to be a sign
for future generations; when their children would
ask, "What do these stones mean to you?", they could
rehearse the miracles of crossing into their Promised
Land (Josh. 4:6).

Again, it is not difficult to grasp the lesson in
God's command to create memorials. Yet I do not
feel we have fulfilled that command as well as we
should have. God has moved in every generation in
unique ways and using unique vessels; He has also
worked miracles in all believers' lives simply by
redeeming us. There is no stronger witness to the
supernatural power of God than the personal

testimony of one who has been redeemed. Future generations need to be able to ask, "What do your stones mean to you?", and then receive an answer that will teach them the ways of God.

I am not referring to building monuments to a movement or a person; that could border dangerously on idolatry. But to point the way to God by teaching those who follow us the supernatural ways in which God has led us can only inspire them to properly fear Him and desire to follow Him as well.

## Fulfilling the Covenant

God was faithful continually to give Joshua the next command that the nation of Israel needed to prepare them for the battles that lay ahead of them. The next instructions could have taken Joshua off guard, however. Now that all of Israel was encamped in the Promised Land, they were actually occupying enemy territory. That could have been cause for some nervousness, at least among this multitude that was uninitiated to the rigors of war.

> *There is no stronger witness to the supernatural power of God than the personal testimony of one who has been redeemed.*

It was here that the Lord told Joshua to circumcise the sons of Israel. These fighting men were the sons of the men of war who came out of Egypt, and they had not been circumcised in the wilderness. It seemed untimely, however, to incapacitate the men at this juncture, sitting as they were in enemy territory. They would be defenseless for several days because of the time that it would take for them to heal.

Yet God required this cutting of the flesh at their most vulnerable time in order to roll away the reproach of Egypt from them (Josh. 5:9). The New Testament clearly refers to the "circumcision of heart" that is necessary for believers:

> But he is a Jew, which is one inwardly; and circumcision is that of the heart, in the spirit, and not in the letter; whose praise is not of men, but of God.
>
> —ROMANS 2:29, KJV

> In whom also ye are circumcised with the circumcision made without hands, in putting off the body of the sins of the flesh by the circumcision of Christ.
>
> —COLOSSIANS 2:11, KJV

You will not see your promised land without allowing the Holy Spirit to cut away the fleshly desires that would militate against your obeying the commands of your Lord. Those carnal tendencies do not desire the things of God, as the New Testament clearly teaches in Romans 7, and will not submit to the rigors of warfare required to possess your promised land. As you look more closely at the enemies in the land, which have their counterpart in the "flesh," you will understand more clearly why you need to submit to the circumcision of your heart, the separation of your fleshly desires from those of your spirit. Again, it is the Word of God that will make this possible:

> For the word of God is living and active and sharper than any two-edged sword, and piercing as far as the division of soul and spirit, of both joints and marrow, and able to judge the thoughts and intentions of the heart.
>
> —HEBREWS 4:12

Joshua was commanded in Joshua 1:8 not to let the book of the law depart from his mouth, but to meditate on it day and night and to be careful to obey it. This commandment is true for us also. Not only will our obedience to it serve to separate the soulish from the spiritual within us, but it will also help us to receive by faith the promised land God desires to give to us. In that way we will make our way prosperous and have good success.

*You will not see your promised land without allowing the Holy Spirit to cut away the fleshly desires that would militate against your obeying the commands of your Lord.*

The apostle Paul renounced the New Testament believer's involvement in physical circumcision as a means for salvation, declaring:

> For in Jesus Christ neither circumcision availeth anything, nor uncircumcision; but faith which worketh by love.
>
> —GALATIANS 5:6, KJV

Faith is the key to walking in divine destiny. And faith works by love. The Bible teaches that faith comes from hearing the Word of God and that we love God because He first loved us (Rom. 10:17; 1 John 4:19). Loving God and loving the Word of God must be synonymous in your life if you desire to enter your promised land. To the degree that you allow your heart to be circumcised from the world and your own fleshly desires, you will find your passion for God and your courage to obey His Word increase.

These preparations for war were imperative for Israel, and they are imperative today as well. Though you do not fight against flesh and blood, you do war against principalities and powers that would like to keep you from enjoying the victory God has ordained for you (Eph. 6:12). Experiencing the supernatural guidance and power of God, creating a memorial of that reality and allowing your heart to be circumcised from all that would hinder your progress are necessary preparations for possessing your promised land.

## THE CAPTAIN OF THE HOST OF THE LORD

Your dependence on God increases as you move toward your destiny. That dependence is not comfortable for your "flesh," because your flesh likes to be in control. Yet there is growing confidence in your heart that because God is *with* you and *for* you, you will indeed possess your promised land. Over and over God declared that He was *giving* the children of Israel their Promised Land. He would drive out their enemies and let them enjoy their inheritance.

Joshua's dramatic encounter with God on the eve of their first battle reinforced that truth for him and for all Israel. He was simply preparing for war, along with the others, and happened to look up to see a man standing nearby with his drawn sword in his hand. Joshua did not recognize the man, so he went to him and asked, "Are you for us or for our adversaries?" (Josh. 5:13).

The answer he received to his question left no doubt as to whom he was talking to: "No, rather I indeed come now as captain of the host of the LORD" (v. 14). Whether it was the force of the words or the supernatural power of His presence, the impact of this warrior's presence caused Joshua to fall on his face before him and, in stark recognition, ask, "What has my lord to say to his servant?" (v. 14).

> *Loving God and loving the Word of God must be synonymous in your life if you desire to enter your promised land.*

The Lord told Joshua to remove his sandals because he was standing on holy ground, and Joshua did so (v. 15). There are few more powerful worship scenes in the whole of Scripture. Such a visible manifestation of the King of kings must have settled all questions in Joshua's mind regarding the outcome of the imminent battle against Jericho, or for the entire war, for that matter. We know it was the Lord because even angels do not allow men to bow before them in an attitude of worship; worship is reserved for God alone.

You can expect similar divine "invasions" when you are facing the enemies that inhabit your promised land. It is God's desire to give you the land, and He is prepared to do battle for you and with you—but never without you—until His promise is fulfilled in your life. Your willingness and obedience, your faith and love, are all that are required to inherit your promised land. In your weakness, His supernatural power will be made manifest; the victory is sure. Don't focus your eyes on the enemy of your soul; instead, look to the Captain of the Lord's hosts, and you will not fail to inherit your promised land.

Chapter 4

# Recognizing an Aggressive Enemy

*Be of sober spirit, be on the alert. Your
adversary, the devil, prowls about
like a roaring lion, seeking
someone to devour.*
*—1 Peter 5:8*

I n any kind of war, the most crucial element of successfully defeating the enemy is the ability to recognize him—his nature, his weapons and his strength. Intelligence reports are extremely helpful in the United States military in determining who our enemy is and how we may best wage war to defeat him. As you look briefly at the enemies the Israelites faced in order to possess their Promised Land, you can gain valuable insight into the nature of your enemies, which would threaten to keep you from your promised land. You can learn from them, as well, the battle strategy you need to defeat them. Israel understood that there were seven nations living in their Promised Land. They had been told clearly who their enemies were by name:

> When the LORD your God shall bring you into the land where you are entering to possess it, and shall clear away many nations before you, the Hittites and the Girgashites and the Amorites and the Canaanites and the Perizzites and the Hivites and the Jebusites, seven nations greater and stronger than you.
> —DEUTERONOMY 7:1

## SIGNIFICANCE OF ENEMIES' NAMES

You may be aware that names were very significant in these ancient civilizations; they were filled with meaning that revealed the character and nature of a person. For example, Abram's name means "high or exalted father."[1] God visited him and changed his name to Abraham, which means "father of a multitude" (Gen. 17:5).[2] Abraham's name was prophetic of the role he would play in God's great plan to have a family.

Jacob's name means "cheater, supplanter."[3] You know from his story that he lived up to that name, cheating his brother out of the birthright and the blessing, among his other deceptive behavior recorded in the Scriptures. When Jacob wrestled with the angel of the Lord, the angel asked Jacob to declare his name. When he did, the angel said he would no longer be called Jacob, but Israel, which means "prince or ruler with God"(Gen. 32:28).[4] The study of names in the Scriptures reveals many wonderful truths regarding the nature and character of people, along with the purpose of God for them.

> *The most crucial element of successfully defeating the enemy is the ability to recognize him—his nature, his weapons and his strength.*

Similarly, the names of these enemy nations reveal their character and nature, from which we can draw parallels to help us identify enemies that occupy our promised land. The "spirits" of these enemies are still very present today, exerting their influence and strength to defeat God's people, both individually as believers and corporately as the church.

## THE CANAANITES

All of the peoples dwelling in the land of Canaan were referred to as Canaanites. These nations were descendants of Canaan, son of Ham, son of Noah (Gen. 9:25). However, the people of one of the seven nations were specifically called Canaanites, as well. They dwelt in the lowland by the sea and by the coast of Jordan (Num. 13:29).

Their name is possibly derived from the Hebrew word *kana,* referring to a low place and also containing the idea "to depress" or "humiliate."[5] These people were content to live in the lowlands as merchants and traffickers (Isa. 23:8). Hosea refers to "a merchant, in whose hands are false balances, he loves to oppress" (Hos. 12:7). That word for *merchant* can also be translated "Canaanite."[6]

Eager for monetary gain through deception and unwilling to exert the effort necessary to live on a higher plain, this selfish, covetous spirit is easily recognizable today. The Canaanite spirit is manifested in all of our flesh; none of us are exempt from it. This spirit whispers its lies to try to satisfy you with the lowlands. After all, you are in the land of Canaan; you are a Christian, what more could you want? You don't need to progress any further. This spirit convinces you to live camped just inside the gate, beneath your privileges in God.

Of course, the Canaanite spirit can sound reasonable. Perhaps you are convinced that you don't deserve anything more from God, considering your past. After all, you were a real sinner, and you are grateful to have your sins forgiven and know you are going to heaven. This Canaanite enemy tries to humiliate and depress you using whatever argument it can. You may feel inferior and believe that God would not hear your prayers, or you decide to stay in the lowlands of depression because of a relative who wants to live there.

Recognizing this "lowland" mind-set as an enemy is the first step in defeating it. God's promises are available to all of His children; you can have all of the promised land you want to have. The Lord gave that promise to Joshua: "Every place on which the sole of your foot treads, I have given it to you" (Josh. 1:3). Instead of running to and fro seeking material gain and living for the temporal, you need to leave that low place of existence and seek to possess more of the land that is promised to you in God. Rather than allow the condemning voice of this enemy to taunt you with the past or convince you that you are inferior, you need to be strong and courageous to stand against its lies.

*The Canaanite spirit convinces you to live just inside the gate of Canaan, beneath your privileges in God.*

Joshua was given specific instructions to meditate on the law of God day and night in order to be

successful in possessing the promise (Josh. 1:8). In
that same way, you need to learn to wait on the Lord
in order to defeat the dishonest, selfish and lazy
Canaanite spirit that wars in your flesh against your
spirit. The Scriptures are filled with promise to those
who learn to wait on the Lord. The prophet Isaiah
declared:

> Those who wait for the LORD will gain new
> strength; they will mount up with wings like
> eagles, they will run and not get tired, they will
> walk and not become weary.
>
> —ISAIAH 40:31

What a contrast to the lowlander's mentality—
mounting up with wings like eagles! If the enemy
can convince you that you are a "chicken" that must
simply peck around in the barnyard, even when you
have been given the powerful wings of an eagle,
you will not take the initiative to mount up above
the trees and soar over the mountains. Deception is
a powerful tool the enemy wields to keep you living
beneath your privilege in God. As you choose to
wait on the Lord, you will become convinced of
who you are in Christ, and with faith rising in your
heart, you will drive out the humiliating, lowland
enemy. Begin to declare the truth of God as the
Scriptures reveal to you who you are:

> I can do all things through Him who
> strengthens me.
>
> —PHILIPPIANS 4:13

> In all these things we are more than con-
> querors through him that loved us.
>
> —ROMANS 8:37, KJV

## THE AMORITES

The Amorites were the biggest nation Israel had to conquer. They lived in the hill country and were considered mountaineers. Their dominance was not felt simply because of their sheer numbers, however. The character of these peoples, according to the derivation of their name, is described as boastful and proud, and they enjoyed a sense of "publicity" in their prominence.[7]

The name *Amorite* derives from the Hebrew *amar,* which means "to say," with a wide range of possible connotations, including boasting, challenging, demanding and speaking against.[8] This enemy nation involved many cities and kings that had to be defeated, as we will see. By virtue of their name, we understand that these enemies work in teams; only in that way can they communicate their proud ideas and speak their lies to each other. Because of their strength, they love to taunt and belittle those who are not a part of them.

This enemy nation blatantly bears the character of Satan, whom Jesus called the father of lies (John 8:44). They do not know God, so they do not dwell in truth. They do not know the Word of God, which is truth. It is not difficult to recognize this enemy spirit in the world today; it dwells in every unbeliever. They have no knowledge of the truth and are boastful, proud and filled with blasphemous "words."

Sadly, Christians have not dealt with this enemy as they should, putting it to death and not tolerating it in their lives. How many churches have been almost destroyed by the backbiter and gossip, the slanderer and talebearer? To slander a person simply means to attack the reputation of another. The Scriptures characterize a person who slanders as a fool: "He who conceals hatred has lying lips, and he who spreads slander is a fool" (Prov. 10:18).

> *Until we acknowledge that we are one in Christ, the glory of God will not be revealed. And the Amorite spirit does its best to keep disunity in the church.*

There seems to be nothing that men pay less attention to than their words; yet nothing is as important. We are identified by our words. The apostle James made this clear:

> If anyone thinks himself to be religious, and yet does not bridle his tongue but deceives his own heart, this man's religion is worthless.
>
> —JAMES 1:26

As enemies of God, these Amorites are characterized as talkers; they like to talk, but their talk is empty. Many times they are liars. There are people in the church who have to be heard, whether it is to tell a dream or vision or to give advice. You need to be on guard for that proud spirit. I am not against prophecy or visions—I have been taught by them. But I am concerned about truthfulness. The Amorite spirit does not cooperate with the spirit of truth. When the spirit of truth moves in, this spirit has to leave. Truth will set you free. The apostle Paul instructed the Colossians:

> Lie not one to another, seeing that ye have put off the old man with his deeds; and have put on the new man, which is renewed in knowledge after the image of him that created him.
> —COLOSSIANS 3:9–10, KJV

We need to separate ourselves from the Amorite spirit in people we may even call friends, but who are talebearers and gossipers. They are the people who congregate and cause a church split, then go down the road and start another church. This enemy must be exterminated from the church. God is going to cleanse the body of Christ and have a unified church. The Scriptures teach that there is one nation, one Father, one body, one blood. Until we acknowledge that we are one in Christ, the glory of God will not be revealed. And the Amorite spirit does its best to keep disunity in the church.

One evening when I was preaching, I heard the Holy Spirit say through my lips, "I will not, I will not, I will not allow anyone who has touched My program, My prophecy, My plan or My prophets to go into the land; they will die and bleach their bones in the wilderness." We are living in the greatest hour there has been in the history of the world. The Word of God is flowing in revelation more pure and in greater volume that ever before. Truth is flowing; our eyes are opening to the purposes of God.

The church is being cleansed from these enemies that have tried to defeat us. God is going to have a pure church; He is cleansing our temples and filling our mouths with words of truth and the power of God instead of gossip and criticism. Negative, unbelieving, lying tongues cannot possess the promised land. We have bowed to those enemies long enough. Jesus made clear the kind of words that should flow out of us:

> He that believeth on me, as the scripture hath said, out of his belly shall flow rivers of living water. (But this spake he of the Spirit, which they that believe on him should receive: for the Holy Ghost was not yet given; because that Jesus was not yet glorified.)
>
> —John 7:38–39, kjv

Living water represents the words of life that we are to receive from the Holy Spirit and speak to one another and to unbelievers. The New Testament teaches that we are to be sanctified by the washing of water by the word (Eph. 5:26–27), in this instance referring to water as a type for the Word of God. That passage continues to say that in this way Christ will present to Himself a glorious church without spot or wrinkle by cleansing us through His Word.

When Peter preached on the Day of Pentecost and three thousand souls were saved, he demonstrated that living water pouring out of his innermost being. We will become the Word of God as living waters flow out of our bellies (John 7:38). It will be pure water, water for the thirsty to drink. We will be identified by our words—words of life that bring the truth of God to lost souls. We must learn to be truth bearers so that people can receive eternal life.

Recently I began to understand more clearly that God's people are a people of truth—out of them run rivers of living water. God said, "I want you to become the Word." The Bible is going back home, but not on India paper. You are walking epistles— walking Bibles. The church is going to be full of the Word. The Word is going back

*Unless you deal with the Amorite spirit that speaks its filth in so many ways, you will not release the living words of life within you.*

home. It...He...the Word of God...left home (John 1). He...It...is going back in us. He writes it on the tablets of our heart. The Word is going back home where He was before the beginning. We are walking epistles read of all men (2 Cor. 3:2). What is the gospel according to us?

Unless you deal with the Amorite spirit that speaks its filth in so many ways, you will not release the living words of life within you. Instead, you will be robbed of faith by this enemy as it speaks its unbelieving words, filled with strife and unlove. I encourage you to recognize the work of this enemy in your life and declare him to be defeated. Fill your mind and your mouth with the living Word of God, and you will begin to walk in victory as you possess your promised land.

## THE HITTITES

Have you wondered why our society seems to be growing more violent every day? The news is filled with violent acts of crime against innocent people. The media has become obsessed with producing violent programs, which they say they do because people want to see that kind of dark, malevolent programming. The Scriptures are clear that the one who desires to kill, steal and destroy is the devil. Jesus came to bring life and life more abundantly (John 10:10). The archenemy of that abundant life is the one who promotes death. One of the tribes the nation of Israel had to face characterizes this evil desire to oppress and violently overthrow their victims.

They were called the Hittites, and they dwelt in the mountains of upper Syria (Num. 13:29). They were a powerful, warlike nation whose name means "terror, fear, great dread." It originates from a word that meant "to prostrate"; hence it signifies to break down either physically, by violence, or by confusion and fear, oppressing and discouraging their victims.[9]

The Hittite spirit vexes, nags, accuses, tantalizes and terrifies those it attacks. It can attempt to overcome the Christian by bringing him or her under the yoke of people who are ruled by this terrorizing spirit, hindering them from walking in the joy of the Lord. Of course, Satan is characterized as the accuser of the brethren (Rev. 12:10). And he tries to bring confusion and torment to the minds and hearts of believers. He also works overtime in the church to sow seeds of discord and bring believers under his control.

This spirit accuses, tantalizes, discourages and terrifies. If it wars within you, before you realize it, you have spent fifteen minutes thinking about something negative and accusatory toward yourself or others. This spirit first accuses God; second, it will accuse the Word; third, it will accuse the brethren; and fourth, it accuses you. It may deceive you into thinking it is bringing conviction, as the Holy Ghost does. There is nothing holy about this spirit. It doesn't convict; it only condemns. The Holy Ghost doesn't do that. "The fruit of the Spirit is love, joy, peace, patience, kindness, goodness, faithfulness, gentleness, self-control" (Gal. 5:22–23). He comes to correct gently and bring His conviction with hope of forgiveness and deliverance.

The Hittite spirit vexes and nags—convincing you that you will never do anything right, that you don't

have what others have in God. That is true; you
don't. You have what God gave you. My heavenly
Father told me one night, "I don't have a copy
machine." He said, "I don't run a duplicator. I don't
even make a hundred special vessels just alike, as
collectors' items. When I make a vessel, I make only
one." You are not supposed to be like someone else;
you are an original in God. How many times have I
wished to be like someone else—I have lamented
that I can't preach like someone else. God said, "I
didn't intend for you to. You are unique—there is
just one like you." And God has a special promised
land for you.

This Hittite argument may sound something like,
"Why do you think God would use you?" He will
enforce fear of failure
when you attempt to
obey God's revealed
purpose for your life.
Or he will accuse you
of wrong motives,
convincing you that
ambition is the ruling
drive of your life,
which is not pleasing
to God. Creating an
atmosphere of fear and terror, he defeats many
Christians by binding them with these chains.

> *The Scriptures are clear that the one who desires to kill, steal and destroy is the devil. Jesus came to bring life and life more abundantly (John 10:10).*

Christians cannot be happy and carefree if they
are filled with fear and torment from their evil

accuser. The Scriptures confirm that fear has torment (1 John 4:18). It was fear that caused Peter to
sink when he saw the wind and the waves, though
he was walking on water toward the Master. Fear
hinders your prayer life as well as your testimony.
The Scriptures declare that the fear of man brings a
snare (Prov. 29:25). You are trapped in unbelief and
defeat when you cringe in fear before men or devils.

We cannot possess our promised land unless we
wage war against this enemy. I am not talking about
something illusory—I am talking about our land,
the wonderful purpose of God for our lives.
These "ites" dwell in our temples, our hearts and
minds. We did not ask them to live there; we
inherited them when we were born. When we
were delivered from Egypt, which is a type
for sin, we were born again to salvation and inherited a promised land that is flowing with milk and
honey. But there are enemies that dwell there, which
we must dispossess in order to enjoy the blessings of
God on our lives.

We have followed God through a wilderness that
became a place of discipline, training and testing.
And we have submitted to the circumcision of our
hearts, choosing to follow Christ wholeheartedly

> Christians cannot be
> happy and carefree if
> they are filled with fear
> and torment from their
> evil accuser.

and giving up any desire for the world. Every place the sole of our foot treads, every enemy that we conquer, takes us farther into the destiny and divine purpose of God for our lives. To change the metaphor, we have chosen to become the temple of God, cleansing it from every unclean thing that would defile it.

This is not a vague kind of symbolism. The children of Israel went into a physical land of property and dirt, their Promised Land, that was filled with enemies that were too strong for them. That physical land is a type of the land we live in—our temple of clay. God has placed His treasure in our clay:

> But we have this treasure in earthen vessels, that the excellency of the power may be of God, and not of us.
>
> —2 CORINTHIANS 4:7, KJV

Unfortunately, within our earthen vessels there are enemies, which we must defeat as surely as the Israelites had to defeat these powerful tribes, if we are going to realize the power of God living through us. Too often we want everyone else to be delivered of their "ites," but we want to keep ours. We recognize the evil of their "ites," but ours are pets—we have had them ever since we got here—we got them from Grandpa and Grandma—they have our names on them. We don't recognize them as enemies. They are part of our personality. We say, "That is just the way we are."

It is important to recognize these enemies and understand that they will keep you from inheriting your promised land. Though you are saved through the blood of Christ, that is not the end of His work in you. You told pharaoh he wouldn't see you any-more—you were headed for the promised land. You wanted to get there in a few days, and so did the children of Israel. But the Bible tells us that if they had gotten there, they would have been destroyed because they were not ready to fight. They did not know war, and these nations would have destroyed them. God took them a long way around because He had to do a work in them before He could give them their inheritance.

If you are tired of living on an emotional roller coaster, fighting the same battles with fear and unbelief over and over, it is time to recognize your enemy and determine to possess your promised land. Dwelling in a place as a camper, without owning any-thing, is different from possessing it. Salvation from sin and living in your inheritance are two different states of being. These enemies will keep you from possessing the promises God has ordained for you to have, fulfilling His divine destiny for your life. Only

> *It is important to recognize these enemies and understand that they will keep you from inheriting your promised land.*

as individual believers rise up against these enemies will the church be cleansed so that it can be filled with the glory of God.

Although the Canaanites, Amorites and Hittites are formidable enemies, as we have seen, because of their overt tactics to defeat believers, their counterparts—the Hivites, Perizzites, Jebusites and Girgashites—may seem even more overwhelming in their shrewd, deceiving ways. As you determine to defeat the violent Hittite spirit and choose to conquer the evil-speaking Amorite, as well as overrule the demeaning lowlander Canaanite spirit, you will need to seek God's divine deliverance for these more subtle, conniving enemies as well.

Deception is one of the primary ways Satan works his destruction in the lives of well-meaning Christians. He began in the garden with the first woman, tempting her to doubt the word of God with his taunt, "Has God said?" (Gen. 3:1). His half-truths and blasphemous taunts tempted Jesus in the wilderness as well, but the Master knew that this evil one could not stand against the truth of the written Word. Jesus understood that the primary weapon against deception is the truth of the Word of God.

However, Satan has continued his deceiving work in the world, destroying many who have not recognized his lying ways or understood that their only safe place is to stand in the truth of the Word. This deceptive work of the enemy is not unrelated to the Amorite spirit, which speaks vanities, emptiness and things contrary to the truth. But its subtlety gives deception a particular strength in that it can innocently masquerade as a legitimate way of reasoning the truth.

## THE HIVITES

The Hivites were an enemy tribe living in the Promised Land that seemed quite innocent, peace loving and even life giving, as their name indicates. The name *Hivite* comes from a word that means "life-giver."[1] It is the Hebrew word for *Eve*, the mother of all living. (By implication, it referred to an encampment or village of tents, a people who were interested in family and in multiplication of flocks and herds rather than war.)

These peace-loving, family-oriented people learned to use cunning persuasion and diplomacy to gain their objectives, as the history of several of their cities records for us. There is a story involving a Hivite nation in Genesis that helps to characterize for us the warmhearted, impulsive and overconfident nature of this enemy. It is a rather distasteful incident that involved the Hivite prince, Shechem, who assaulted Dinah, the daughter of Jacob. Shechem saw her and desired her and then defiled her. Instead of fighting for her, he persuaded his father to go and ask Jacob to give her in marriage, offering whatever dowry would be necessary for the negotiation. In spite of this warm attempt at diplomacy, the sons of Jacob, angered because of what had happened to their sister, showed their father's strength of deception in their shrewd response. They declared that Shechem could not have their sister unless every man of this pagan nation was circumcised.

These Hivite men agreed to fulfill this prerequisite for the marriage of Shechem to Dinah. However, when the men were sore and were healing in their

> *The primary weapon against deception is the truth of the Word of God. the living words of life within you.*

tents, the sons of Jacob pursued them and killed every one because their sister had been defiled. Jacob was frightened that the Hivites would seek revenge. But it perhaps confirms their unwarlike nature that their Hivite neighbors did not make any attempt at revenge against Jacob and his family. (See Genesis 34:2–31.)

There were many cities of Hivites, one of which was Gibeon (Josh. 9:7, 17). The Gibeonites showed special cunning and deceit to avoid the slaughter that God had commanded of the Israelites to all of the enemies living in the Promised Land. The Gibeonites also showed a foresighted keenness and disposition to persuade by means of diplomacy rather than by arms. Theirs seems to have been a rather democratic rule of law, judging by the reference to "our elders and all the inhabitants of our country" who had instructed them in their ploy to make a covenant with Joshua (Josh. 9:11).

There is no other tribe that makes me as angry as this one. They are so wrapped up in what seems to be "good" that we don't recognize them as enemies. In their deceptive diplomacy, the Gibeonites sent out envoys who pretended to live very far away. In their ingratiating way, they told Joshua that they wanted to make a covenant with Israel, since they lived so far away and had heard "of the fame of the LORD your God" (v. 9). They knew what God had done to the kings of the Amorites, and so their elders told them to make the long journey to ask

Joshua to make a covenant with them. They must have been convincing, because the Scripture declares that Joshua believed them and made a covenant with them (v. 15).

The Scripture says plainly that the men of Israel did not ask for the counsel of the Lord in their decision to make a covenant with the deceptive Gibeonites (v. 14). And Joshua made peace with these enemies, entering into a covenant of compromise, only to discover that they were neighbors. When he discovered his error, it was too late; they could not break their covenant made before God that they would not destroy them. They had to find a way to live with these enemies the rest of their lives. They determined to make them slaves, drawers of water and hewers of wood for all of Israel. Though they had to live as slaves the rest of their days, these deceptive enemies succeeded in saving their lives in the face of God's command that they be destroyed.

Disobedience to the command of God to utterly destroy all of the enemies that lived in Canaan opened Israel to deception by these cunning enemies. Joshua didn't even recognize this tribe as an enemy. The strong implication for his failure is that he did

> Hivites are so wrapped up in what seems to be "good" that we don't recognize them as enemies.

not seek counsel of the Lord. A closer analysis of this enemy will help you to recognize him in your life. This enemy tries to get your pity and attention. The end result is that he will leech on to you in order to save his life, causing you to compromise the blessing of God on yours.

Especially if you are a sincere believer who wants to help others, this ingratiating spirit can appear as a person who needs your counsel. Before long, he involves you in his deceptive web of lies. He needs all of your attention; he will die if you don't help him. You are the "savior" of this self-pitying victim who is willing to make a covenant with you as long as you will give him what he needs. You need to point these misguided people to God and encourage them to cultivate a personal relationship with Him in prayer and in dedication to His Word. They will find truth if they seek it and be delivered by the power of the Holy Spirit.

You may find it as difficult to identify this enemy in your life as it was for Israel to recognize the Gibeonites as enemies. They seemed peace loving, willing to pacify any demands of a holy God for their destruction. Their feigned innocence earned them a "right" to live though their death had been decreed by God. This enemy may appear in your life as a distraction that you did not seek God about. You may be bound to seemingly legitimate relationships or possessions or even recreational activities that rob you of time with God. They distract you from your focus on the purpose of God for your life, thereby leeching from you the power to possess your promised land.

Jesus declared that the truth would set us free (John 8:32). If you seek God regarding all of your involvements, He will be faithful to reveal to you any deceptive attachments or distractions that are causing you to live in compromise and are keeping you from possessing your inheritance. I have always maintained, personally, that there is nothing and nobody who is worth my missing what God has ordained for me. Don't be fooled by these peace-loving, self-legitimatizing enemies that pursue you to make a life covenant with them, bringing death to your destiny.

> *If you seek God regarding all of your involvements, He will be faithful to reveal to you any deceptive attachments or distractions that are causing you to live in compromise and are keeping you from possessing your inheritance.*

## THE GIRGASHITES

We know that the Girgashites were named among the tribes who lived in the Promised Land who were to be utterly destroyed by Israel. And it is believed they were in possession of the land east of the Sea of Galilee. Some scholars identify the Girgashites with the Gadarenes of the capital city, Gadara. Otherwise, their name is from an obscure patrial root, its meaning unknown.[2] We do know that the nations that inhabited Canaan were idolatrous peoples, building altars to pagan gods, so we will focus on this aspect of this enemy in our discussion.

That the Girgashites were among those who built graven images is documented by the Scripture:

> And when the LORD thy God shall deliver them before thee; thou shalt smite them, and utterly destroy them; thou shalt make no covenant with them, nor shew mercy unto them: Neither shalt thou make marriages with them; thy daughter thou shalt not give unto his son, nor his daughter shalt thou take unto thy son. For they will turn away thy son from following me, that they may serve other gods: so will the anger of the LORD be kindled against you, and destroy thee suddenly. But thus shall ye deal with them; ye shall destroy their altars, and break down their images, and cut down their groves, and burn their graven images with fire.
>
> —DEUTERONOMY 7:2–5, KJV

God cannot tolerate idolatry, the making of graven images or bowing down to other gods, because He is God; there is none beside Him. And He knows the innate power of idolatry to lead His people astray. He warned His people not to allow their children to marry the youth of these pagan nations, because they would turn them away from serving God. That is why they were told not to make any covenant with them, as they did with the Gibeonites. Their presence makes us vulnerable to their idolatrous influence, which brings us under the wrath of God.

While it may be difficult for you to recognize idolatry in your life, you need to be careful that you are not defeated by the idolatrous ways of "innocent" enemies that accost you. They may appear as friends or family who urge you not to be too radical or go too far in your consecration to Christ. They counsel you not to be a fanatic—just giving you advice that will keep you from "losing your mind." When people talked to me that way, I just told them that I was trying to lose my mind so that I could have the mind of Christ.

*High-minded thoughts pose as friendly, caring considerations when in reality they are intent on ruling your life, whether they come from others or find residence in your own mind.*

High-minded thoughts pose as friendly, caring considerations when in reality they are intent on ruling your life, whether they come from others or find residence in your own mind. Scripture is clear that you need to allow your mind to be transformed and renewed by the Word of God so that you will not be conformed to this world (Rom. 12:1–2). Otherwise, it is naturally hostile to the will of God and filled with love for self and for the world (Rom. 8:7). Love of the world represents a subtle form of idolatry that divides your affections from your covenant relationship with God.

The apostle Paul indicted Demas, saying that he loved this present world and deserted the work of the Lord (2 Tim. 4:10). And the elder John declared bluntly:

> Do not love the world, nor the things in the world. If anyone loves the world, the love of the Father is not in him. For all that is in the world, the lust of the flesh and the lust of the eyes and the boastful pride of life, is not from the Father, but is from the world. And the world is passing away, and also its lusts; but the one who does the will of God abides forever.
>
> —1 JOHN 2:15–17

The lust of the flesh that John listed, by definition, involves many aspects of our natural life:

- ∾  Our appetites
- ∾  Our passions
- ∾  Our sensual indulgence

- Our drives for power, position and possessions

The lust of the eyes can affect us in the following ways:

- Love of things
- The way we dress
- The whole pageant of worldly display of "beauty"

The pride of life, which is perhaps the highest form of worldliness, can be recognized in:

- Pride of family, ancestry, race
- Pride of culture
- Pride of intellectual ability, talent
- Pride of power
- Pride of ministry

While these lists are not meant to be exhaustive, they will help you think about your own values and perhaps discover idolatrous areas that are hiding in your mind and heart. You need to recognize the idolatrous nature of your self-life in order to defeat it and inherit your promised land.

The antidote for your tendency to the idolatry that lies in your flesh is found in Galatians 5:16: "This I say then, Walk in the Spirit, and ye shall not fulfil the lust of the flesh" (KJV). I was praying about that one day, and I asked my Father what He meant about commitment and dying to self. He spoke to me, "To the degree you are willing to give up your will, your way, your words, your walk, your worship and your warfare, you can have Mine."

That is not just an alliterative statement; it expresses the reality of your need to abandon your life to God, area by area and degree by degree, dying to yourself so that you can inherit the promises of God.

You don't do it all at once. Death to self is gradual. The crucified life involves coming to the cross as you would go to a swap shop, an exchange counter. It is a sacred place where you swap off your junk that you thought was so precious. You may say, "Surely God doesn't want me to give that up." Yes, He does. Whatever threatens the supremacy of your relationship with Christ must be exchanged for His life; it is an idol.

I don't own anything. Have you ever walked through your house and said to God, "This is not mine—it is Yours"? What is it you would hold on to rather than have that exchanged for Him? The crucified life is not negative; it is a positive deliverance of your junk to get His righteousness. It is getting rid of what you were born with as a result of sin in exchange for what He wants you to be, and He provides for your keeping.

I questioned why the Lord wanted my junk. I said, "What can You possibly do with what I have? I don't have anything compared to what You have."

He said to me, "You can't have what I have if I can't have what you have."

He may destroy it or He may use it, but it is not yours—it is His. I felt as if I was standing in His glorious presence with dirt and filth, like trash—like what I had was nothing—to look in the face of almighty God and come to exchange what I have for His glory. When you see Him in His glory, giving up what you have is not hard. He wants to empty you so that He can fill the temple with His glory.

We are talking about possessing the land—not Canaan, but your soul—where you live your life in this temple of flesh. There is a vast difference in living in the land and possessing it. Some have lived in the lowlands and never moved any higher. They are content to say, "I am saved, washed in the blood; I am going to heaven," and they are offended if you talk to them about

> *"To the degree you are willing to give up your will, your way, your words, your walk, your worship and your warfare, you can have Mine."*

moving further. The Bible says that every foot of ground you put your foot on shall be yours. Let me encourage you to denounce your enemies and declare, "Move out, Satan; move out, flesh."

The worst enemy you have is not the devil. We rebuke the devil a lot over things that "we are."

There is a person inside of you called "I." The person you sleep with, the one who wears your clothes, the one you sign your name as, is the worst enemy you have. Your heart is idolatrous until you submit to the lordship of Christ. Only then can you begin to recognize the enemies of your flesh that would keep you from inheriting your promised land. Jesus lives inside of you; God houses Himself inside of you. And yet you hang on to who you are when you could have who He is.

You are a free moral agent. God doesn't take anything away from you; you have to bring it to the cross and give it up. As I mentioned, this is a process; you don't die all at once. For years I believed a doctrine of sanctification that said once and for all, in a moment, we could be totally delivered from the "I" in us. The only thing wrong with that faulty doctrine is that when I thought I had died to my self-nature, the next morning she was sitting at the foot of my bed to greet me.

There is a reality to being sanctified, but it is a reality only to the degree that you allow His holiness to become yours. There is a moment in time when you build an altar, deliberately and willfully, and, to the best of your knowledge, say an eternal *yes* to God. You determine to be separate and holy unto God and never again willingly say *no* to Him. It is that total commitment that brings fire to your altar. But time will be a necessary element, as it was with Israel, to rid your "land" of all the enemies residing in it. To the degree that you allow that nature to die, you will live in your inheritance. It is so wonderful to get rid of more of that nature, but don't be surprised when you think you have gotten rid of him and he appears again. Remember, there were seven different tribes that lived in Canaan, along with many kings in many cities of the land.

The apostle Paul admonished the Philippians to "let this mind be in you, which was also in Christ Jesus" (Phil. 2:5, KJV). Part of your divine inheritance is a right to receive revelation from God. It is knowing how God thinks—understanding the Word as He wrote it, not as you may have learned it from someone else. It is allowing Him to take this Book and write it on the tablets of your heart. You don't have to beg Him to do that; you are to "let" His mind be in you. Having His mind will fill you with His purpose and His desires, unfolding your personal destiny as you possess your promised land.

*The crucified life is not negative; it is a positive deliverance of your junk to get His righteousness.*

When we talk about the glory of God, we need to remember that every temple that man ever built for God in the Scriptures, He filled with His glory when they met the requirements of dedication to God. But He never intended to live in those temples. They were makeshift physical buildings where He could appear to commune with mankind. According to the New Testament, we are the temple of God that He wants to live in (1 Cor. 6:19). He is intent on cleansing our temples, as Jesus did in Jerusalem, from moneychangers and other idolatrous inhabitants. His temple shall be a place of prayer, as Jesus declared. When we make our temples a place of prayer and praise, power and purity, He will fill us with His glory. As He fills believers with His presence, the church will be filled with the glory of God.

This is an hour when revelation is flowing. God is speaking His Word even through children and young people. The apostle Paul prayed for the Ephesians a prayer that is significant for the church today:

> For this reason I too, having heard of the faith in the Lord Jesus which exists among you, and your love for all the saints, do not cease giving thanks for you, while making mention of you in my prayers; that the God of our Lord Jesus Christ, the Father of glory, may give to you a spirit of wisdom and of revelation in the knowledge of Him. I pray that the eyes of your heart may be enlightened, so that you may know what is the hope of His calling, what are the riches of the glory of His inheritance in the saints, and what is the surpassing greatness of His power toward us who believe.
>
> —Ephesians 1:15–19

Of course, the Scriptures were inspired by the Holy Spirit. The Holy Ghost—the divine teacher, the intercessor whose prayers cannot be reversed— prayed that we have a spirit of revelation. Why? So that we could know the hope of His calling and the riches of the glory of His inheritance in the saints. We have been discussing our inheritance in God. But can you fathom the wonder that the infinite God has an inheritance in you? There is no greater treasure than to have God share His mind with you—taking the Word off the pages until it becomes your life. Then out of your mouth will run rivers of living water.

This wonder of divine revelation is your inheritance. And the prophet Isaiah declared that the knowledge of the Lord is going to cover the earth as the waters cover the sea (Isa. 11:9). Out of our vessels, temples of God, His knowledge is going to flow like rivers of water. When that flow of revelation comes, as a result of our cleansing, Christ is going to have a church filled with His glory.

*Part of your divine inheritance is a right to receive revelation from God. It is knowing how God thinks— understanding the Word as He wrote it, not as you may have learned it from someone else.*

Idolatry will be defeated when the glory of God

reigns. And the converse can also be stated: When idolatry is defeated, the glory of God will reign.

## THE PERIZZITES

Though there is little known about the ancestry of the Perizzites, they were evidently some of the original inhabitants in the land. They seem to have occupied the woods and hills south of Palestine as well as the area to the western side of Mt. Carmel (Josh. 17:15–18).

The name *Perizzite* refers to an inhabitant of the open country or people who dwell in unwalled villages.[3] This is an interesting characterization of a people who were content to be squatters, without owning their land or building protected cities as was the custom of the day.

We can conclude that they were an indolent, drifter society without proper restraints on their lives. They wanted to be "free" to wander about the land, but they did not take care to protect their own or take ownership in order to be responsible to build a thriving community.

Unfortunately, this Perizzite spirit is quite common today, even among Charismatics. We call them "church hoppers"—they flit from one congregation to another, never committing to become a part of the body of Christ to help build a local church with their giftings. Or they feed on messages they hear from one conference to another—unwalled, but unproductive as well. It is difficult to grow in faith and character when you live to yourself, moving with the wind and not being accountable to any kind of spiritual authority.

The apostle Peter admonished believers to "grow in the grace and knowledge of our Lord and Savior Jesus Christ" (2 Pet. 3:18). And the apostle Paul taught clearly our responsibility to the body of Christ:

> That we henceforth be no more children, tossed to and fro, and carried about with every wind of doctrine, by the sleight of men, and cunning craftiness, whereby they lie in wait to deceive; but speaking the truth in love, may grow up into him in all things, which is the head, even Christ: from whom the whole body fitly joined together and compacted by that which every joint supplieth, according to the effectual working in the measure of every part, maketh increase of the body unto the edifying of itself in love.
>
> —EPHESIANS 4:14–16, KJV

It is interesting that the Scripture is so clear as to your responsibility to be joined to the body of Christ and to work effectively together so that the body can be edified in love. These Perizzite enemies did not represent that lifestyle, yet they were allowed to live also in the land of Canaan after the conquest under Joshua. The results were disastrous. They entered into marriages with their conquerors and seduced the Israelites into idolatry

(Judg. 3:5–6).[4] You dare not choose to live your Christian life without becoming an active part of a local body of Christ, His church, if you expect to inherit your promised land. The selfish motivation that wants to be "free" of any accountability or proper restraint will defeat you and cause you to be a slave to the idolatry of your own flesh life.

I believe a revival is coming that will cleanse the church of all of these seductive "ites." The Holy Ghost is cleansing the church and delivering it so that God might inhabit it eternally. We are going to possess the land that Christ died to give us. We are not going to marry the ites; we are going to conquer them.

My Father told me to go to the church and look for leaders and help them get ready to lead the church into the promised land where we have never been. In the type of Canaan, Israel went into a physical land, which represents our inheritance in the spirit. But they did not possess all of the land. And they did not drive out all of the enemies that lived there.

> When we make our temples a place of prayer and praise, power and purity, He will fill us with His glory.

The Lord told me to get leaders ready to lead His people into the promised land. He said that our heavenly Joshua—Jesus—is going to take the church into her inheritance. He is going to clean it and deliver it and take it to the Mount of Transfiguration. He is going to let the glory of God be revealed in the church, and all flesh shall see it. The whole earth shall see the glory of God. I'm not talking about some cloud or pillar of fire; the glory of God is the manifested, visible presence of the omnipotent God. This world is going to see Jesus in the church.

There is one more enemy to conquer in the promised land, one that inhabits the Holy City itself.

## THE JEBUSITES

The Jebusites, the last nation mentioned that lived in the land of Canaan, were mountaineers, living in the "hill country" (Num. 13:29; Josh. 11:3). Their city was Jerusalem (Josh. 15:63), also known as Jebus.[5] Their warlike character is seen throughout their entire history. It was Adonizedek, king of Jerusalem, who raised the confederacy against Gibeon (Josh. 11:1, 3).

*It is difficult to grow in faith and character when you live to yourself, moving with the wind and not being accountable to any kind of spiritual authority.*

Their name *Jebusite* means an inhabitant of Jebus, and comes from a root word that means "to trample, literally or figuratively, with an understanding of loathing and treading down under foot."[6] Though the king of Jerusalem was among those smitten by Joshua (Josh. 12:10), the Jebusites still retained at least their royal city (Judg. 1:21) until the time of David (2 Sam. 5:6–8; 1 Chron. 11:4–6). The Scripture says, "Now as for the Jebusites, the inhabitants of Jerusalem, the sons of Judah could not drive them out" (Josh. 15:63).

Whatever the reasons, these enemies of God's people, who were supposed to be destroyed, proved to be too strong for them. Hundreds of years later, after David was anointed king, he led his army against the Jebusites. And David made this former enemy stronghold, now called the City of David, the capital of his kingdom. Yet, even when David finally captured the fortress of Jebus, the inhabitants were spared, and they continued to inhabit the temple hill.

The tenaciousness of this proud enemy along with its strategic location, dwelling in the city of God, the holy city that is so significant to events of Bible history and to future events as well, makes it a formidable foe. Its tactic is to wear you down, to drain your strength, appearing to be impossible to conquer. It is entrenched in an impenetrable fortress and is intent on treading underfoot anything that threatens its domain. It is a proud foe, dominating in power because of its impenetrable nature.

This tribe wears you out. It seeks to take your strength. You are too tired to pray, and always too tired to go to church. This spirit does not want you to have strength enough to climb the mountains. We sing about eagles, but we must live in the mountains as eagles to soar the way they do. If the enemy can get you in the lowlands to live in a barnyard and wear you out with his fortified attacks, he will keep you from inheriting your promised land. You need to see the greatness of God to fight for you against the most formidable enemies.

We are about to experience a new revelation of who our God is that is going to bring a new reverence and respect for the power of God. We are instructed in Scripture to dance before the Lord, but there are times as well that we need to bow in worship. How big is our God? I don't mean what kind of miracles He can perform. How awesome is He? How holy is He? Too many Christians have made Him a "Santa Claus" who brings us the new toys we ask for. He is our Daddy, but He is also God. The church has lost a sense of reverence for God. I am not talking about dead churches where silence reigns; I am talking about being in awe of the presence of God—so we won't trifle with the presence of God. It is the nature of pride to bring God down to "our level."

When Gypsy Smith was living, he came to Greensboro, North Carolina, where I was living, and I was privileged to hear him speak. When he stood to read the Scriptures, an usher came down the aisle to open a window overhead with a long tipped with a hook. Gypsy Smith stopped and waited for the usher to finish his task. Then he said, "God's Word is about to be read." His reverence for the Word of God would not allow him to read while someone was doing a mundane task. We need to regain that sense of awe for the holiness of God, His Word,

> *We are about to experience a new revelation of who our God is that is going to bring a new reverence and respect for the power of God.*

prayer and worship. As we see Him for who He is, almighty God, we will be able to climb the mountain in faith to defeat our strongest enemy.

The proud-spirited Jebusites tread down and trample underfoot whatever interferes with their plans and purposes. Pride originated in the heart of Satan, which resulted in his being cast out of heaven. The prophet Isaiah records the evil desire that took root in Lucifer's heart:

> But you said in your heart, I will ascend to heaven; I will raise my throne above the stars of God, and I will sit on the mount of assembly in the recesses of the north. I will ascend above the heights of the clouds; I will make myself like the Most High.
>
> —ISAIAH 14:13–14

The desire to be the supreme authority in your life, making your own decisions and doing things your way is paramount to saying, "I will ascend," or "I will make myself like the Most High." When you fail to acknowledge the lordship of Christ in your life, you are becoming your own god; self is enthroned in your heart and mind. That is the chief enemy in your life that will keep you from pos-

> *As we see Him for who He is, almighty God, we will be able to climb the mountain in faith to defeat our strongest enemy.*

sessing your promised land. It is that proud spirit that tramples other people who get in your way or threaten your goals. It is the thought that you know what will make you happy and the attitude that no one can tell you what to do.

The Book of Proverbs tells us that God hates pride:

> These six things doth the LORD hate: yea, seven are an abomination unto him: a proud look, a lying tongue, and hands that shed innocent blood, an heart that deviseth wicked imaginations, feet that be swift in running to mischief, a false witness that speaketh lies, and he that soweth discord among brethren.
>
> —PROVERBS 6:16–19, KJV

You might think the enemy of pride would be easy to recognize and that when we see how it is working in our own hearts we would hate it and get rid of it. But that is often not the case. While it may be easy to see the high mindedness working in other people, we rarely see how it works in our own mind. One of the ways we can recognize pride is to test our attitudes and actions by the Word of God.

The Scripture declares, "The wicked, through the pride of his countenance, will not seek after God: God is not in all his thoughts" (Ps. 10:4, KJV). Pride keeps us from seeking God. We sometimes say that we are too busy or too tired to spend time in the Word or cultivate a devotional life with the Lord. But according to the Word of God, it is pride that goes its own way without thinking of God.

And pride manifests itself in the way we think of others. The apostle Paul was teaching the Philippians to cultivate the humility of Christ when he wrote:

> Do nothing from selfishness or empty conceit, but with humility of mind let each of you regard one another as more important than himself; do not merely look out for your own personal interests, but also for the interests of others.
>
> —Philippians 2:3–4

Paul continued by describing the greatest humility that ever existed: God becoming man—Christ—and humbling Himself to death on the cross (Phil. 2:5–8).

I believe we will spend eternity trying to fathom the wonder of the Incarnation, but we can experience the humility of Christ in our hearts as we yield to His life within us. He will defeat the strong prideful spirit that deceives our own minds and keeps us from possessing the promised land He wants us to experience.

The more we experience victory over this tribe, the more we know it is God's grace and glory delivering us. When we are delivered from their influence, we learn to live in humility—and we find rest for our souls. Jesus invited us to find this rest:

> Come unto me, all ye that labour and are heavy laden, and I will give you rest. Take my yoke upon you, and learn of me; for I am meek and lowly in heart: and ye shall find rest unto your souls. For my yoke is easy, and my burden is light.
>
> —MATTHEW 11:28–30, KJV

To overcome these seven evil spirits, you need to follow God's instructions for His strategy to use against them. You need to tear down their altars and burn their images. And you must never make a covenant with them to allow them to live. As you search the truth of God's Word and relate to the body of Christ, the deceptions of

*Self is the chief enemy in your life that will keep you from possessing your promised land.*

these cunning enemies will be exposed, and you will be able to defeat their purposes in your life. And, little by little, you will see God's power drive them out, allowing you to enjoy your promised land.

Chapter 6

# A WINNING BATTLE STRATEGY

*Therefore, Hebron became the inheri-
tance of Caleb the son of Jephunneh the
Kenizzite until this day, because he followed the* LORD *God of Israel fully.*

—JOSHUA 14:14

Only two men who left Egypt, according to the Scriptures, went into the Promised Land. Joshua and Caleb were among the twelve men Moses chose to spy out the land. The other ten spies came back and gave a negative report about the giants that lived there, causing the people's hearts to melt in fear. Joshua and Caleb declared the beauty of the land and that God would make the giants bread for them.

Because of the Israelites' unbelief, God let them wander in the desert until they died. Their children would inherit the Promised Land meant for them to enter. But because Caleb followed the Lord fully—wholeheartedly—along with Joshua, they were allowed to inherit the Promised Land. His was a winning battle strategy—complete abandonment to God. Even his physical strength had not abated during the forty years in the wilderness. He declared:

*The winning strategy for inheriting your promised land involves yielding to the Holy Spirit at every point.*

> So Moses swore on that day, saying, "Surely the land on which your foot has trodden shall be an inheritance to you and to your children forever, because you have followed the LORD my God fully." And now behold, the LORD has let me live, just as He spoke, these forty-five years, from the time that the LORD

spoke this word to Moses, when Israel
walked in the wilderness; and now behold, I
am eighty-five years old today. I am still as
strong today as I was in the day Moses sent
me; as my strength was then, so my strength
is now, for war and for going out and coming in. Now then, give me this hill country
about which the LORD spoke on that day, for
you heard on that day that Anakim were
there, with great fortified cities; perhaps the
LORD will be with me, and I shall drive them
out as the LORD has spoken.

—JOSHUA 14:9–12

God was with Caleb and drove out the enemy,
giving him his inheritance in Hebron, which had
been the stronghold of the strongest of the Anakim,
giants, in the land. The winning strategy for
inheriting your promised land involves following
the Lord wholly, yielding to the Holy Spirit at every
point where your will, your thoughts and your
desires differ with His divine purpose for your life.
The Holy Spirit comes to dwell in your spirit, filling
you with the life of God. He will express that divine
life through your soul—your mind, emotions and
will. When God's will becomes your will, His
thoughts your thoughts and His desires your
desires, you can say with the apostle Paul:

I have been crucified with Christ; and it is no
longer I who live, but Christ lives in me; and
the life which I now live in the flesh I live by

faith in the Son of God, who loved me, and delivered Himself up for me.

—GALATIANS 2:20

## THIRTY-ONE KINGS

In Joshua 12 there is a list of thirty-one kings that the Israelites defeated. They were rulers of cities belonging to the seven tribes we have discussed, and each one is named and counted. Their lands were distributed among the tribes of Israel as they overcame these enemies of God. I encourage you to read the accounts of how God fought for Israel, intervening in the battles and giving them the winning strategies they needed. Your own faith will grow to believe that He will do the same for you.

The old nature that clings to us seems to have as many "kings" as those that ruled in the land of Canaan. Our self-life does not die easily. A. B. Simpson assigned a "face" of self for each one of the thirty-one kings listed in Joshua 12 that the Israelites defeated, and I am sure his list is not exhaustive.[1] I challenge you to ask the Holy Spirit to show you which of these kings are living in your "land."

### 1. Self-will

The head of the "self" dynasty, it expresses its decrees in the personal pronoun and the active verb, "I will, I shall."

### 2. Self-indulgence

This is the gratification of self in any of its forms.

### 3. Self-seeking

Love seeks not her own; her object is not to accomplish some personal end, but to benefit another and to glorify God.

### 4. Self-complacency

This is the spirit of pride that takes delight in our own qualities and rests with satisfaction in ourselves.

### 5. Self-glorying

The converse of self-complacency, self-glorying seeks the praise of others rather than its own. It vaunts itself and inflates its little bubble because it is so small.

### 6. Self-confidence

This is a form of self-life that relies upon its own wisdom, strength and righteousness. It is filled with common sense and self-reliance.

### 7. Self-consciousness

This is the self that is always thinking of itself; every act, look and word is studied, morbidly photographed upon the inward senses.

### 8. Self-importance

Some carry this in their gait and bearing, making up for their lack of real weight by an immense amount of self-assertion and swaggering assumption. True humility consists not so much in thinking meanly of ourselves as not thinking of ourselves at all.

### 9. Self-depreciation

Some people are overly conscious of their own shortcomings and inability, which keeps them from useful service and is always thrusting its littleness and nothingness upon every situation.

### 10. Self-vindication

This is the self that stands for its own rights and avenges its wrongs. It is quick to detect an injury or an offense and to express its sense of it in some marked and unmistakable way.

### 11. Sensitiveness; touchiness

This is one of the most painful forms of selfishness.

### 12. Self-seeing

This perspective always sees things from its own side, asking, *How does this affect me?*

### 13. Introspection

Morbid and excessive self-examination is one of the forms of self-life that causes much pain and works much injury in our Christian life. God alone can truly search us.

### 14. Self-love

This is the root of all forms of the self-life; it is a heart centered upon itself, and as long as this is the case, every affection and every power of our being is turned inward and self-ward.

## 15. Self-affections

These are the natural fruit of self-life—our own friends and families and the people who minister to our pleasure, whom we love for the pleasure they minister to us rather than the blessing we can be to them.

## 16. Selfish motives

Our selfish motives may enter into the highest acts and mar and pervert them to their inmost core. God judges our acts by their intent, not only what we say and do, but why.

## 17. Selfish desires

The spirit of covetousness is just a selfish desire. God has pronounced it idolatry and most dreadful sin, always springing up in the old natural heart.

## 18. Selfish choices

These are more serious than selfish desires, for the will is the spring of human actions and determines our words and deeds.

## 19. Selfish pleasures

These pleasures we seek for their own sake, seeking our own that terminates on itself. True enjoyment comes to us from doing good in harmony with God, which is the truest enjoyment.

## 20. Selfish possessions

The worldling seeks to gain the world and calls his possessions his own; the true Christian conception of property is stewardship, the holding of the gifts of God for His service and subject to His direction and for His glory.

### 21. Selfish fears and cares

Nearly all our cares and anxieties spring from pure selfishness. If we were yielded to God, we would have no anxiety, but would regard ourselves as His property under His safe and constant protection.

### 22. Selfish sorrows

These are griefs from wounded pride, ambition, self-love or the loss of something that we should not have called our own.

### 23. Selfish sacrifices and self-denial

To make sacrifices or deny self for the gratification of vanity or the display of orthodoxy and the propagation of your own beliefs and opinions is simply the old stream of life turned into a new channel.

### 24. Selfish virtues and morality

Unwilling to do what the good Samaritan did for the fallen victim, selfish virtue is a cloak, intended for display and therefore worthless.

### 25. Self-righteousness

This face of self would seek to justify itself before God by its own religious works, and thus forfeit His righteousness and salvation.

## 26. Selfish sanctity

Becoming so absorbed in our religious experience that our eyes are taken off Jesus, we become offensive exhibitions of religious self-consciousness. True sanctification forgets itself and lives in constant dependence upon the Lord Jesus.

## 27. Selfish charities

The largest generosity may be only an advertisement of ourselves, prompted by some motive that terminates on our own interest or honor.

## 28. Selfish Christian works

We may preach or work for the church because we like the church, the minister or the people, or we may do our religious work from religious selfishness.

## 29. Selfish prayers

Prayers of many Christians travel in a circle about the size of their own body and soul, their family and church; the highest prayer is the prayer of unselfish love for a dying world.

## 30. Selfish hopes

The future of many persons is as selfish as their present, filled with dreams of coming joys and triumphs that are earth-bound.

## 31. Selfish life

Our very life must be held not as a selfish possession, but as a sacred trust, as the apostle Paul understood when he said, "For to me to live is Christ, and to die is gain" (Phil. 1:21).

## Surrender: The Key
## to Conquest

God is faithful to exchange your sinful nature for His divine nature as you determine to bring these "faces" of your self-life to the cross. A. B. Simpson asks and answers these important questions:

> How shall we overcome these giants? How shall we win the victory over self? We must surrender ourselves so utterly that we can never own ourselves again. We must hand over self and all its rights in an eternal covenant, and give God the absolute right to own us, control us and possess us forever. We must let God make this real in detail, as each day brings its tests and conflicts. We must receive the great antidote to self—the love of Christ. And finally, we need not only the love of Christ but Christ Himself. It is not a principle, nor an emotion, nor a motive, that is to transform our life and conquer these determined foes, but it is a living Person.[2]

Christ has made it possible for you to lose your self-life entirely and enter into the freedom of eternal life as you become a partaker of His divine nature. The apostle Peter declared this truth triumphantly:

> …His divine power has granted to us everything pertaining to life and godliness, through the true knowledge of Him who called us by

His own glory and excellence. For by these He
has granted to us His precious and magnifi-
cent promises, in order that by them you
might become partakers of the divine nature,
having escaped the corruption that is in the
world by lust.

—2 PETER 1:2–4

Possessing your inheritance involves the ability to
live a holy life and receive impartation of the divine
nature as you contin-
ually give yourself to
God and learn to truly
know Him. He makes
it possible for you to
become a partaker of
the divine nature,
delivering you from
the corruption of this
generation. As you
study His Word,
humbly seeking Him, you will begin to think as He
thinks; you will exchange your worldly thoughts for
His kingdom thoughts.

> *Christ has made it possible for you to lose your self-life entirely and enter into the freedom of eternal life as you become a partaker of His divine nature.*

The Holy Spirit will cause the written Word to
live to you, and Christ, who is the Word, will
become your life. You will realize the reality of what
the apostle Paul wrote: "Christ in you, the hope of
glory (Col. 1:27). As I wrote in my book *Placed in
His Glory:*

The work of the Holy Spirit is to reveal the

glory of Jesus in us. As long as we are in control, He can't be. The "I" nature wants to rule, having my way and exercising my rights, never allowing the Holy Spirit to do what He came to do. If we take our "I" to the cross, we can exchange it there for the I AM. Then the Holy Spirit moves into every area of our personality, and the veil of flesh begins to fall away. We begin to realize that we don't think as we used to think. The truth will dawn on us: "These aren't my thoughts." Then we understand Paul's injunction to "Let this mind be in you which was also in Christ Jesus" (Phil. 2:5)...

The Holy Spirit begins to replace Adam's carnal mind with the mind of Christ so we can think as our Daddy thinks. Then He changes our rebellious wills as well. As we keep surrendering to the Holy Spirit, He begins to take the Father's will that we know nothing about and move into our wills. He makes our wills His will and His will our will, if we say yes to Him. As we yield to the Holy Spirit's work within us, we begin to walk with God and to become the will of God.[3]

Perhaps you will never fully grasp the wonder of redemption, even throughout all of eternity. But you can rejoice in it and experience the reality of the life of Christ in you—your promised land—as you abandon yourself to the Holy Spirit within you. He has come to change you into the image of Christ, causing this "treasure in earthen vessels" to shine forth, "that the excellency of the power may be of God, and not of us" (2 Cor. 4:7, KJV). And He made your victory possible:

> And when you were dead in your transgressions and the uncircumcision of your flesh, He made you alive together with Him, having forgiven us all our transgressions, having canceled out the certificate of debt consisting of decrees against us and which was hostile to us; and He has taken it out of the way, having nailed it to the cross. When He had disarmed the rulers and authorities, He made a public display of them, having triumphed over them through Him.
> —COLOSSIANS 2:13–15

Christ did it all for us. Why should we be defeated by enemies that seem too strong for us—our anger, our self-pity or our pride? We must be very courageous to put off the old man and put on the new, as Paul admonished us:

> …in reference to your manner of former life, you lay aside the old self, which is being corrupted in accordance with the lusts of deceit, and that you be renewed in the spirit of your mind, and put on the new self, which in the likeness of God has been created in righteousness and holiness of the truth.
> —EPHESIANS 4:22–24

Chapter 7

# Enjoying Your Inheritance

*But as it is written, Eye hath not seen,*
*nor ear heard, neither have entered into*
*the heart of man, the things which God*
*hath prepared for them that love him.*
—1 Corinthians 2:9, kjv

We cannot conclude our study without focusing on life as God ordained it in the Promised Land. Can you more clearly answer the question we asked at the beginning: What is your promised land? Do you know what it looks like? Is there a growing desire within you to pursue it and let nothing hinder you from inheriting what God has promised? So, what does your promised land look like?

For the Israelites, the land of Canaan became their homeland where they could raise their families and worship their God. According to Bible historians, the land was a pleasant land and exquisitely beautiful. There were mountains—not craggy, rocky and barren, which are frightful to the traveler and useless to the inhabitants—but fruitful hills, such as put forth precious things, which charmed the spectator's eye and filled the owner's hand (Deut. 33:15). And valleys, not mossy and boggy, but covered with corn (Ps. 65:13). There were plains and springs to water them. Even in that rich land there were wildernesses too, or forests, which were not so thickly inhabited as other parts, yet had towns and houses in them; these served as foils to set off the more pleasant and fruitful countries.[1]

God promised the children of Israel a land flowing with milk and honey at the same time He told them about their enemies:

And I am come down to deliver them out of

the hand of the Egyptians, and to bring them up out of that land unto a good land and a large, unto a land flowing with milk and honey; unto the place of the Canaanites, and the Hittites, and the Amorites, and the Perizzites, and the Hivites, and the Jebusites.

—Exodus 3:8, kjv

And He promised not only to give them a wonderful land in which to live, but also to drive out their enemies before them (Exod. 33:2). Their part was to seek Him for the battle strategy, obey His commands and to utterly destroy every one of their enemies in the divine power He would give them. Of course, the Scriptures record that Israel did not fully obey the Lord in possessing their land; they did not destroy all of their enemies. But their inheritance was based on the land they did conquer through disposing of their enemies.

*Our promised land is characterized by freedom from our enemies—enemies in our self-life of oppression, pride and every other "king" that wars against our souls, robbing us of peace and prosperity.*

For New Testament believers, the promised land is not a physical territory; it is a spiritual one. While Jesus did promise houses and lands to those who left all to follow Him (Mark 10:29–30), these do not represent the promised land He came to give us. Our promised land is characterized by freedom from our enemies, as we have discussed—enemies in our self-life of oppression, pride and every other "king" that wars against our souls, robbing us of peace and prosperity.

Jesus taught us to pray, "Thy kingdom come. Thy will be done on earth as it is in heaven" (Matt. 6:10). And the Scriptures declare that "the kingdom of God is not eating and drinking, but righteousness and peace and joy in the Holy Spirit" (Rom. 14:17). Allowing the kingdom of God to come to "my" earth—this earthen vessel—will result in a life of righteousness filled with peace and with joy. Those will be characteristics of our promised land.

All of God's promises can be yours, as part of your promised land, when you choose to overcome the enemies that would keep you from inheriting it. Even the psalmist understood the spiritual reality of this promised land when he declared, "As for me, I will behold thy face in righteousness: I shall be satisfied, when I awake, with thy likeness" (Ps 17:15, KJV). Fulfillment is to be found only as you behold the face of God, and in beholding Him, you are changed into His likeness. Again, the psalmist described this place of exquisite satisfaction when he wrote:

> Thou wilt make known to me the path of life; in Thy presence is fulness of joy; in Thy right hand there are pleasures forever.
>
> —PSALM 16:11

When you have defeated your enemies and are possessing the promises of abundant life God has given you, you will experience the fulfillment of your personal destiny and enjoy the intimate relationship with God, which brings rest to your soul.

Your promised land does not only involve your fulfillment individually, however. God intends, as He did with the nation of Israel, to show forth His glory in the church corporately. As the character of God is released through the lives of believers corporately, He will have a glorious church without spot or wrinkle (Eph. 5:27). The righteousness of God will be manifest in His church, along with His peace and His joy. There is an aspect of the glory of God that involves a manifestation of His visible presence that is peculiar to the church corporately. Like a diamond that reflects and refracts rays of light, the church is filled with believers shining forth in facets of light. It was the apostle Peter who declared of the church:

*As believers learn to defeat the enemies of their souls and inherit their promised land, unity will be birthed in the church.*

> But ye are a chosen generation, a royal priesthood, an holy nation, a peculiar people; that ye should shew forth the praises of him who hath called you out of darkness into his marvellous light: Which in time past were not

> a people, but are now the people of God:
> which had not obtained mercy, but now have
> obtained mercy.
>
> —1 PETER 2:9–10, KJV

God's glory must be manifested in the personal holiness of each believer. It is multiplied synergistically when those believers form the corporate expression of Christ in the church. God's glory must be revealed in the power of each believer's transformed life, those who have possessed their promised land. In the context of the church, as individual temples of clay release the treasure that is within them, God's glory is going to fill the earth.

As believers learn to defeat the enemies of their souls and inherit their promised land, unity will be birthed in the church. No longer will Christians be self-seeking; they will esteem others better than themselves (Phil. 2:3). No longer will they insist on their own way or live for self-glory; they will serve one another in love. And Jesus prayed that when the world would see that kind of unity, they would be drawn to Him:

> That they all may be one; as thou, Father,
> art in me, and I in thee, that they also may be
> one in us: that the world may believe that thou
> hast sent me. And the glory which thou gavest
> me I have given them; that they may be one,
> even as we are one: I in them, and thou in me,
> that they may be made perfect in one; and that
> the world may know that thou hast sent me,

and hast loved them, as thou hast loved me.
—John 17:21–23, kjv

Part of our promised land will be inherited corporately, as the church of God reflects the glory of God in the earth so that the world will see the love of God.

*Dare to possess your promised land.*

As we possess our personal promised land and the church begins to be filled with the glory of God, I believe we are going to see an old-fashioned, heaven-sent, sky blue, sin-killing, gully-washing revival like the world has never seen. There is going to be a harvest of souls who will want to know our God, the faithful and gracious deliverer of our souls.

While you cannot inherit this promised land all at once, as you saw with Israel, your commitment to obey the commands of God will bring victory, step by step, so that you can possess your inheritance. God Himself promised to fight these enemies of "self" that are too strong for you. As you dare to seek Him, He will reveal them to you and give you the divine strategy to successfully defeat them.

The Scriptures declare that the promised land God has prepared for those who love Him is beyond comprehension:

> But as it is written, Eye hath not seen, nor ear heard, neither have entered into the heart of man, the things which God hath prepared for

them that love him.

—1 CORINTHIANS 2:9, KJV

So go ahead—dare to possess your promised land, and enter into the fullness of God's promises that you never dreamed were possible. He is waiting to reveal the wonders of His life and love to you, in you and ultimately through you, and throughout the church, until His Word is fulfilled:

> For the earth will be filled with the knowledge of the glory of the LORD, as the waters cover the sea.
>
> —HABAKKUK 2:14

# Notes

## CHAPTER 1
### GOD'S PROMISE

1. *Nelson's Illustrated Bible Dictionary* (Nashville, TN: Thomas Nelson Publishers, 1986), s.v. "promise."

2. *The Hebrew-Greek Key Study Bible (NAS): Zodhiates' Original and Complete System of Bible Study,* compiled and edited by Spiros Zodhiates, Th.D. (Chattanooga, TN: AMG Publishers, 1984, 1990).

## CHAPTER 2
### GOD'S PURPOSE IN WAR

1. *Matthew Henry's Commentary on the Whole Bible: New Modern Edition,* Electronic Database. (n.p.: Hendrickson Publishers, Inc., 1991).

## CHAPTER 4
### RECOGNIZING AN AGGRESSIVE ENEMY

1. *Biblesoft's New Exhaustive Strong's Numbers and Concordance with Expanded Greek-Hebrew Dictionary.* Copyright © 1994, Biblesoft and International Bible Translators, Inc., s.v. "Abram."

2. Ibid., s.v. "Abraham."

3. Ibid., s.v. "Jacob."

4. Ibid., s.v. "Israel."

5. Ibid., s.v. "*kana.*"

6. Ibid., s.v. "Canaanite."

7. Ibid., s.v. "Amorite."

8. Ibid., s.v. "*amar*."

9. Ibid., s.v. "Cheth."

## Chapter 5
### Confronting a Subtle Enemy

1. *Biblesoft's New Exhaustive Strong's Numbers and Concordance with Expanded Greek-Hebrew Dictionary*, s.v. "*chavvah*."

2. *Nelson's Illustrated Bible Dictionary*, s.v. "Girgashite."

3. *Biblesoft's New Exhaustive Strong's Numbers and Concordance with Expanded Greek-Hebrew Dictionary*, s.v. "*perazah*."

4. *Nelson's Illustrated Bible Dictionary*, s.v. "Perizzite."

5. *The New Unger's Bible Dictionary*. Originally published by Moody Press of Chicago, Illinois. Copyright © 1988, s.v. "Jebus."

6. *Biblesoft's New Exhaustive Strong's Numbers and Concordance with Expanded Greek-Hebrew Dictionary*, s.v. "Jebusite."

## Chapter 6
### A Winning Battle Strategy

1. A. B. Simpson, *Thirty-one Kings: Or Victory Over Self* (Harrisburg, PA: Christian Publications, Inc., 1992).

2. Ibid.

3. Fuschia Pickett, *Placed in His Glory* (Lake Mary, FL: Charisma House, 2001), 126–127.

### CHAPTER 7
### ENJOYING YOUR INHERITANCE

1. *Matthew Henry's Commentary on the Whole Bible: New Modern Edition,* s.v. "Joshua, chapter 12."

# Enjoy your journey with God!

Dr. Fuchsia Pickett has been referred to as one of the "best Bible teachers of our time," and now you know why!

We pray that you have been inspired with the life message found in *Possess Your Promised Land*, and we know you'll enjoy two more opportunities to sit under her anointed teaching and draw closer to God.

**Step into righteousness.** Uncover God's grace, deliverance, timing and patience. Walk through the seasons of life, and cast aside worldly hindrances.

**Uncover the real meaning of servanthood.** Fulfill your purpose and give thanks for everything God has done, all He is doing now, as well as what He is going to do your future.

Chapter 5

# CONFRONTING A SUBTLE ENEMY

*Even Satan disguises himself
as an angel of light.*
—2 CORINTHIANS 11:14